The Literary Life Commonplace Book

Stories will save the world.

The Literary Life Commonplace Book: Succulent

By Angelina Stanford, Cindy Rollins, and Thomas Banks

Published by Blue Sky Daisies

blueskydaisies.net

ISBN 13: 978-1-944435-12-7

The Literary Life Commonplace Book

This book belongs to:

____.

If found, please contact me at this number:

____.

The Literary Life Podcast Official Commonplace Book
Stories will save the world.

Visit us online at www.theliterary.life.

Subscribe to our podcast.

Join the conversation on our Facebook community:
The Literary Life Podcast Discussion Group

What is a "commonplace book"?

From the Latin *locus communis*, the term "commonplace" refers to a common saying or proverb. Generally speaking, a "commonplace book" is a private collection of proverbs, quotations, and sketches—or anything that catches your interest—that one might keep in a notebook. Although you may wish to jot down your thoughts on various subjects, or sketch out a design you have in mind, literary commonplace books differ from diaries or journals in that they are specifically a place for keeping track of things you are reading or discovering.

From Angelina Stanford

The life of the mind can often feel unreal. I've felt envious of friends who have something tangible to show at the end of their work: paintings, sweaters, a blooming garden. But what do I have to show for the hours I spend with a book in hand? Nothing but thoughts. In 2015, at a time when I very much felt like a wanderer in my own life, I began a new reading journal. I had previously commonplaced rather sporadically. Fits and starts would best describe my efforts. But for the last five years, I have written down every book I have read and the date I completed it. And for the first time, I began to find genuine joy in the process of commonplacing. I luxuriated in the moment of slowing down, reflecting on what I read, contemplating why I wanted to remember this particular quote, and enjoying a sense of accomplishment every time I marked a book completed. Now, when I pick up my journal, I have something tangible to document how I spend my time, and I love thumbing through the pages and seeing a record of what I have read and what I thought about. My commonplace book is a passport bearing the stamps of where I have been in this literary life. I feel less like a wanderer and more like a pilgrim journeying to the holy places.

From Cindy Rollins

I am probably the least traditional when it comes to commonplacing, perhaps because my mother started new notebooks hourly, hiding them so no one would know she was recording her random thoughts and vitamin intake. These days my commonplacing habits include taking pictures of quotes with my phone, underlining things in my Kindle, keeping a file of quotes on Evernote, and adding written quotes to my actual commonplace book every day of the first week of January. Even so, it is jolly fun to keep the same notebook of quotes for many, many years. This January I will be using The Literary Life Podcast journals and I am looking forward to the the common life of sharing my pages and seeing yours too. To misquote an old friend, Kenneth Grahame, whom I have never met, "Believe me, my young friend, there is nothing—absolutely nothing—half so much worth doing as simply messing about in books." I have been messing about in books for a very long time now and commonplacing helps me remember the streams I have visited and the friends I have made whether they are real or not.

From Thomas Banks

"*Books think for me,*" wrote Charles Lamb, and I have come to feel the same way in my own reading life. I first began keeping commonplace books when I was in high school, at the behest of an English teacher. At first I did so half-heartedly, as I did half-heartedly most assigned work at that period of my life. Some years ago, while visiting my parents, I discovered the first such notebook that I kept in a corner of a bookshelf and read through its contents with a growing sense of embarrassment. Most of the entries were, as one might expect, statements and aphorisms of the kind that at the age of fifteen I would have thought profound, or boldly Promethean, or (and these the most comic) "philosophical." The sources from which I had drawn these morsels of wisdom ranged from Byron and Poe to Salinger, and from Sartre ("*Hell is other people.*") to Joe Strummer and Kurt Cobain ("*Oh well, whatever, nevermind.*"). Certain entries reminded me of futile intellectual disciplines I undertook at that age in the desire to appear deeper than I was; one entry from Kierkegaard reminded me of the time I tried to make sense of *Fear and Trembling*, and misunderstood it entirely. Twenty years later, I misunderstand it still.

Somehow the duty became a habit. I continue to keep notebooks full of passages from my reading, partially from a certain odd feeling of closeness to the minds of my favorite authors which I derive from writing out select verses, sentences and paragraphs that are the fruit of their imaginations. The practice is also useful to me in that it supplies a prop to my rather weak memory, through which so much of what I read passes like water through a sieve. So it is that books not only think for me, but remember for me as well.

 Stories will save the world. 

Index

Record the main content of each page here for a handy reference.

Index

39.
40.
41.
42.
43.
44.
45.
46.
47.
48.
49.
50.
51.
52.
53.
54.
55.
56.
57.
58.
59.
60.
61.
62.
63.
64.
65.
66.
67.
68.
69.
70.
71.
72.
73.
74.
75.
76.

 Record the main content of each page here for a handy reference.

Index

Reading Challenge • 20 Books in 2020

20 in 2020 Challenge:	*Title Chosen*	*Completed*
A Shakespeare Play		
A Classic Detective Novel		
A Classic Children's Book		
A Contemporary Novel		
A Historical Fiction Novel		
An Ancient Greek Play		
A Collection of Short Stories		
A Biography or Memoir		
A Devotional Work		
A Book about Books		

 Download a printable list at www.theliterary.life.

Reading Challenge • 20 Books in 2020

20 in 2020 Challenge:	*Title Chosen*	*Completed*
A Foreign (Non-Western) Book		
A "Guilty Pleasure" Book		
An Intimidating Book You Have Avoided		
A Satire		
A Book of Essays		
A Book by a Minor Author		
A Classic Book by a Female Author		
A Complete Volume of Poetry by a Single Author		
An "Out of Your Comfort Zone" Book		
Reread a Book You Read in High School		

Reading Challenge • 19 Books in 2021

192021 Challenge:	Title Chosen	Completed
A Poetry Anthology *Anything from Mother Goose to "Q" (Oxford Book of English Verse by Sir Arthur Quiller-Couch)*		
A Book (or Selection) of Letters		
A Book From Your To-Be-Read Stack		
An Ancient Greek or Roman Work *A play, epic, or collection of myths*		
A Book on Education, Art, or Literature		
A Victorian Novel		
A Lesser-Known Book by a Well-Known Author		
A Shakespeare Play		
A Book You Have Avoided		

 Download a printable list at www.theliterary.life.

Reading Challenge • 19 Books in 2021

192021 Challenge:	*Title Chosen*	*Completed*
Finish a Book You Started but Never Finished		
A Literary Biography		
Something Russian *A play, short story, novel, or novella*		
A Regional or Local Book *A book related in some way to your local area*		
A 14th, 15th, or 16th Century Book *a book written in, set in, or about*		
A Book in a Genre You Don't Normally Read		
An Obscure Book Mentioned by Thomas Banks *Or any book mentioned on the podcast*		
A Light Comedic Novel *Like PG Wodehouse*		
An "Other World" Book		
A Travel Book *(Anything from* Travels with a Donkey *to* A Walk in the Woods*)*		

192021 Kids Challenge:	Title Chosen	Completed
A Book of Myths *Such as* Tanglewood Tales *by Nathaniel Hawthorne*		
Five Fairy Tales *Any selection you like*		
Five Poems by One Poet *Such as Robert Frost, Emily Dickinson, or any other poet*		
Read a Book Aloud to a Sibling or Friend		
A History Biography *Such as Signature Biographies or Landmark or Childhood of Famous Americans or others*		
A Book Recommended by a Grandparent or Older Person		
Ten Fables *Aesop is one author.*		
A Book by an Author You've Never Read Before		
A 19th Century Children's Classic *Such as* The Jungle Book *or* Little Women *or many others*		

Reading Challenge • 19 Kids Books in 2021

192021 Kids Challenge:	*Title Chosen*	*Completed*
A Middle Ages Book *Written in or set in the Middle Ages or Renaissance.* Men of Iron *by Howard Pyle, for example.*		
A 20th Century Children's Classic *The Chronicles of Narnia were written in the 20th century along with many others.*		
A Book You Have Avoided		
Reread a Book		
A Biography of a Composer, Artist, or Writer *You may like Opal Wheeler's artist biographies.*		
Five Tall Tales *American Tall Tales by Adrien Stoutenburg, for example*		
A Book Written or Set in Ancient Greece or Rome		
A Mystery or Detective Novel *Anything from* Encyclopedia Brown *to Dorothy L. Sayers!*		
A Legend *Such as King Arthur or Robin Hood Rosemary Satcliffe writes many books in this genre.*		
A Shakespeare Play *Or a retelling of a Shakespeare play*		

To-Be-Read Stack

Fiction

Title	*Author*	*Recommended by*

Non-Fiction

Title	*Author*	*Recommended by*

To-Be-Read Stack

Read-Alouds

Title	*Author*	*Recommended by*

Poetry

Title	*Author*	*Recommended by*

To-Be-Read Stack

Fairy Tales

Title	*Author*	*Recommended by*

Classic Works

Title	*Author*	*Recommended by*

To-Be-Read Stack

Devotional

Title	*Author*	*Recommended by*

Bestsellers

Title	*Author*	*Recommended by*

Reading Log

Title	*Author*	*Date Read*	*Rating*
			☆ ☆ ☆ ☆ ☆
			☆ ☆ ☆ ☆ ☆
			☆ ☆ ☆ ☆ ☆
			☆ ☆ ☆ ☆ ☆
			☆ ☆ ☆ ☆ ☆
			☆ ☆ ☆ ☆ ☆
			☆ ☆ ☆ ☆ ☆
			☆ ☆ ☆ ☆ ☆
			☆ ☆ ☆ ☆ ☆
			☆ ☆ ☆ ☆ ☆
			☆ ☆ ☆ ☆ ☆
			☆ ☆ ☆ ☆ ☆
			☆ ☆ ☆ ☆ ☆
			☆ ☆ ☆ ☆ ☆
			☆ ☆ ☆ ☆ ☆
			☆ ☆ ☆ ☆ ☆
			☆ ☆ ☆ ☆ ☆
			☆ ☆ ☆ ☆ ☆
			☆ ☆ ☆ ☆ ☆
			☆ ☆ ☆ ☆ ☆

Reading Log

Title	*Author*	*Date Read*	*Rating*

Literary Life Podcast Selections

Title/Author	Podcast	Date Read	My Rating
Gaudy Night Dorothy Sayers	Spring 2019		☆☆☆☆☆
"Araby" James Joyce	Summer 2019		☆☆☆☆☆
"A Defence of Penny Dreadfuls" G. K. Chesteron	Summer 2019		☆☆☆☆☆
"The Garden Party" Katherine Mansfield	Summer 2019		☆☆☆☆☆
"The Adventures of a Shilling" Joseph Addison	Summer 2019		☆☆☆☆☆
"The Necklace" Guy de Maupassant	Summer 2019		☆☆☆☆☆
"Why I Write" George Orwell	Summer 2019		☆☆☆☆☆
"The Celestial Omnibus" E. M. Forster	Summer 2019		☆☆☆☆☆
"The Vulture" Samuel Johnson	Summer 2019		☆☆☆☆☆
An Experiment in Criticism C.S. Lewis	Fall 2019		☆☆☆☆☆
Northanger Abbey Jane Austen	Fall/Winter 2019		☆☆☆☆☆

Literary Life Podcast Selections

Title/Author	Podcast	Date Read	My Rating
A Winter's Tale William Shakespeare	Winter 2020		☆☆☆☆☆
"The Importance of Being Earnest" Oscar Wilde	Winter 2020		☆☆☆☆☆
The Great Divorce C. S. Lewis	Spring 2020		☆☆☆☆☆
"Essay on Education" Simon Weil	Spring 2020		☆☆☆☆☆
"The Trojan Women" Euripides	Summer 2020		☆☆☆☆☆
"On Fairy Stories" J. R. R. Tolkien	Summer 2020		☆☆☆☆☆
"Leaf by Niggle" J. R. R. Tolkien	Summer 2020		☆☆☆☆☆
Till We Have Faces C. S. Lewis	Fall 2020		☆☆☆☆☆
Phantastes George MacDonald	Fall/Winter 2020		☆☆☆☆☆

Literary Life Podcast Selections

Title/Author	*Podcast*	*Date Read*	*My Rating*
Death on the Nile Agatha Christie	Winter 2021		☆☆☆☆☆

Commonplace Quotes

Commonplace Quotes

"A person reveals his character by nothing so clearly as the joke he resents."
—Georg Christoph Lichtenberg in "Aphorisms" (Read by Thomas Banks in Podcast Ep. 72)

Commonplace Quotes

"School isn't supposed to be a polite form of incarceration, but a portal to the wider world."
—Richard Louv in Last Child in the Woods: Saving our Children from Nature-Deficit Disorder *(Read by Cindy Rollins in Podcast Ep. 72)*

Commonplace Quotes

"Milton's point in Paradise Lost *is that free man can be instructed only by the non-compulsive forms, whether vision, parable, or drama. Hence* Paradise Lost *is a series of interlocking visions, Adam warned by the cathartic contrapuntal vision of satanic fall, and fall through vision of Eve. To fall is to choose an illusion, not a wrong reason."*

—Northrup Frye in Notebooks on Renaissance Literature *(Read by Angelina Stanford in Podcast Ep. 72)*

Commonplace Quotes

"There is no truth, however overpowering and clear, but men may escape from it by shutting their eyes."
—Cardinal John Henry Newman in Selected Sermons *(Read by Thomas Banks in Podcast Ep. 71)*

Commonplace Quotes

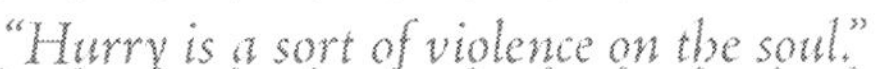

"Hurry is a sort of violence on the soul."
—John Mark Comer in The Ruthless Elimination of Hurry: How to stay emotionally healthy and spiritually alive in the chaos of the modern world *(Read by Cindy Rollins in Podcast Ep. 71)*

Commonplace Quotes

"I should have been shocked in my teens if anyone had told me that what I learned to love in Phantastes *was goodness. But now that I know, I see there was no deception. The deception is all the other way round—in that prosaic moralism which confines goodness to the region of Law and Duty, which never lets us feel in our face the sweet air blowing from 'the land of righteousness,' never reveals that elusive Form which if once seen must inevitably be desire with all but sensuous desire—the thing (in Sappho's phrase) 'more gold than gold.'"*

—*C. S. Lewis in* George MacDonald *(Read by Angelina Stanford in Podcast Ep. 71)*

Commonplace Quotes

"After a certain kind of sherry party, where there have been cataracts of culture but never one word or one glance that suggested a real enjoyment of any art, any person, or any natural object, my heart warms to the schoolboy on the bus who is reading Fantasy and Science Fiction rapt and oblivious of all the world beside."
—C. S. Lewis in "The World's Last Night" (Read by Cindy Rollins in Podcast Ep. 70)

Commonplace Quotes

"Children are not deceived by fairy tales. They are often and gravely deceived by school stories. Adults are not deceived by science fiction. They can be deceived by stories in women's magazines."
—C. S. Lewis in An Experiment in Criticism *(Read by Angelina Stanford in Podcast Ep. 70)*

Commonplace Quotes

"Both fairy stories and realistic stories engage in wish fulfillment, but it is actually the realistic stories that are more deadly. Fairy stories do awaken desires in children, but most often it is not a desire for the fairy world itself. Most children don't really want there to be dragons in modern England. Instead, the desire is for they know not what. This desire for something beyond does not empty the real world, but actually gives it new depths. He does not despise real woods because he has read of enchanted woods. The reading makes all real woods a little enchanted."
—C. S. Lewis in "On Three Ways of Writing for Children" (Read by Angelina Stanford in Podcast Ep. 70)

Commonplace Quotes

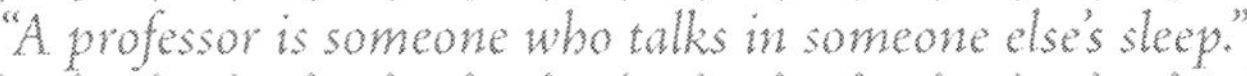

"A professor is someone who talks in someone else's sleep."
—W. H. Auden (Read by Thomas Banks in Podcast Ep. 36)

Commonplace Quotes

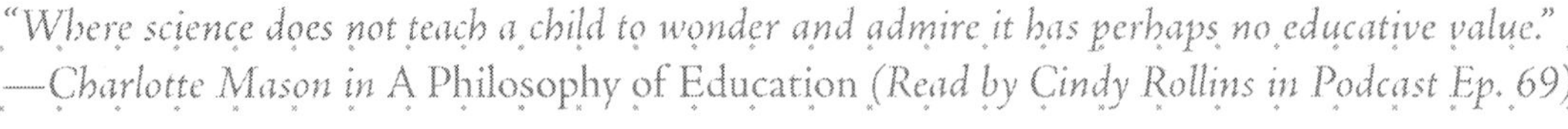

"Where science does not teach a child to wonder and admire it has perhaps no educative value."
—Charlotte Mason in A Philosophy of Education *(Read by Cindy Rollins in Podcast Ep. 69)*

Commonplace Quotes

"Now the story of Christ is simply a true myth, a myth working on us in the same way as the others, but with tremendous difference–that it really happened–and one must be content to accept it in the same way, remembering that it is God's myth, where the others are men's myths. That is, the pagan stories are God expressing himself through the minds of poets, using such images as he found there, while Christianity is God expressing Himself through real things."
—C. S. Lewis in a "Letter to Arthur Greeves October 18, 1931" (Read by Angelina Stanford in Podcast Ep. 69)

Commonplace Quotes

"I can't say I learned nothing at St. Charles Borromeo. I learned bladder control; which is good for women, useful in later life. The second thing I learned was that I had got almost everything terribly wrong."
—Hilary Mantel in Giving Up the Ghost: A Memoir *(Read by Cindy Rollins in Podcast Ep. 68)*

Commonplace Quotes

"We read Dante for his poetry and not for his theology because we have already met the theology elsewhere." —W. H. Auden "D. H. Lawrence" from "The Dyer's Hand and Other Essays" (Read by Thomas Banks in Podcast Ep. 68)

"In the twinkling of an eye, in a time too small to be measured, and in any place, all that seems to divide us from God can flee away, vanish, leaving us naked before Him, like the first man, like the only man, as if nothing but He and I existed. And since that contact cannot be avoided for long, and since it means either bliss or horror, the business of life is to learn to like it. That is the first and greatest commandment."
—C. S. Lewis in God in the Dock *(Read by Angelina Stanford in Podcast Ep. 68)*

Commonplace Quotes

"Hundreds of people can talk for one who can think, but thousands can think for one who can see. To see clearly is poetry, prophesy, and religion. All is one."
—John Ruskin in Sesame and Lilies *(Read by Thomas Banks in Podcast Ep. 67)*

Commonplace Quotes

"Since then I have always been addicted to something or other, usually something there's no support group for. Semicolons, for instance, I can never give up for more than two hundred words at a time."
—Hilary Mantel in Giving Up the Ghost: A Memoir *(Read by Cindy Rollins in Podcast Ep. 67)*

Commonplace Quotes

"The two hemispheres of my mind were in the sharpest contrast. On the one side, a many-islanded sea of poetry and myth; on the other, a glib and shallow 'rationalism.' Nearly all that I loved, I believed to be imaginary. Nearly all that I believed to be real, I thought grim and meaningless."

—C. S. Lewis Surprised by Joy *(Read by Angelina Stanford in Podcast Ep. 67)*

Commonplace Quotes

"This is what I recommend to people who ask me how to get published. Trust your reader, stop spoon-feeding your reader, stop patronizing your reader, give your reader credit for being as smart as you at least, and stop being so bloody beguiling: you in the back row, will you turn off that charm. Stop constructing those piffling little similes of yours."

—*Hilary Mantel* Giving Up the Ghost: A Memoir *(Read by Cindy Rollins in Podcast Ep. 66)*

"The first qualification for judging any piece of workmanship, from a corkscrew to a cathedral, is to know what it is–what it was intended to do and how it is meant to be used."
—C. S. Lewis in Preface to Paradise Lost *(Read by Angelina Stanford in Podcast Ep. 66)*

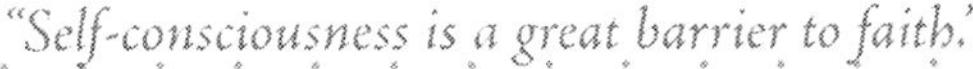
"Self-consciousness is a great barrier to faith."

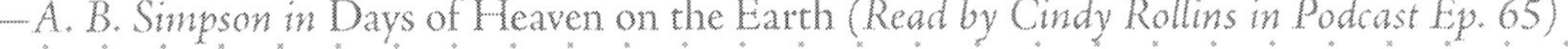
—A. B. Simpson in Days of Heaven on the Earth *(Read by Cindy Rollins in Podcast Ep. 65)*

Commonplace Quotes

"It is a mark of true folklore that even the tale that is evidently wild is eminently sane."
—G. K. Chesterton in "The Common Man" essay collection (Read by Thomas Banks in Podcast Ep. 65)

Commonplace Quotes

"The poet's job is not to tell you what happened, but what happens: not what did take place, but the kind of thing that always does take place."
—Northrup Frye in The Educated Imagination *(Read by Angelina Stanford in Podcast Ep. 65)*

Commonplace Quotes

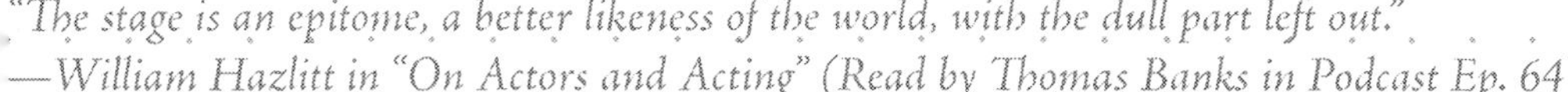

"The stage is an epitome, a better likeness of the world, with the dull part left out."
—William Hazlitt in "On Actors and Acting" (Read by Thomas Banks in Podcast Ep. 64)

Commonplace Quotes

"The motto was Pax, but the word was set in a circle of thorns. Pax: peace, but what a strange peace, made of unremitting toil and effort, seldom with a seen result; subject to constant interruptions, unexpected demands, short sleep at nights, little comfort, sometimes scant food; beset with disappointments and usually misunderstood; yet peace all the same, undeviating, filled with joy and gratitude and love. 'It is My own peace I give unto you.' Not, notice, the world's peace."

—Rumer Godden in In the House of Brede: A Novel *(Read by Cindy Rollins in Podcast Ep. 64)*

Commonplace Quotes

"If I find in myself a desire which no experience in this world can satisfy, the most probable explanation is that I was made for another world...I must keep alive in myself the desire for my true country, which I shall not find till after death;...I must make it the main object of life to press on to that other country and to help others to do the same."

—C. S. Lewis in Mere Christianity *(Read by Angelina Stanford in Podcast Ep. 64)*

Commonplace Quotes

"Riddle: I have eaten the Muses, yet I have profited nothing.
Answer: A bookworm."
—Symphosius in a book of Latin Riddles (Read by Thomas Banks in Podcast Ep. 63)

Commonplace Quotes

"In our culture of betrayal, we are quick to impose our own views on layers of established systems. Thus, even a work of art is to be distrusted. Rather than trying to "under-stand" the work, we stand over it and dismiss it as unreadable. Or worse yet, we impose a critical ideology upon it without first allowing the work to affect us."
—Makoto Fujimura in Refractions *(Read by Cindy Rollins in Podcast Ep. 63)*

Commonplace Quotes

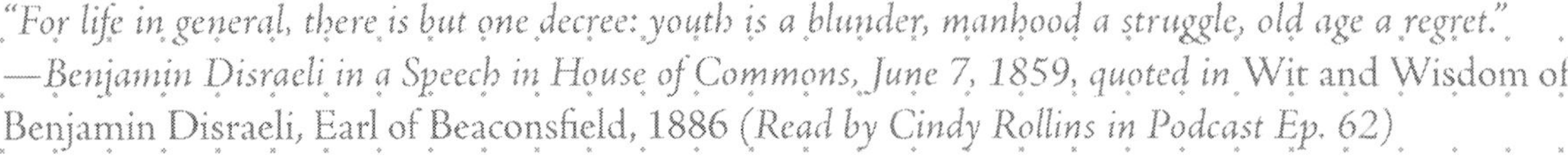

"For life in general, there is but one decree: youth is a blunder, manhood a struggle, old age a regret."
—Benjamin Disraeli in a Speech in House of Commons, June 7, 1859, quoted in Wit and Wisdom of Benjamin Disraeli, Earl of Beaconsfield, 1886 *(Read by Cindy Rollins in Podcast Ep. 62)*

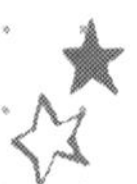

Commonplace Quotes

"I replied: 'My dear Alphonse, men in those olden days had convictions, we moderns have only opinions; and something more than mere opinion is necessary to the erection of such a Gothic cathedral.'" —Heinrich Heine in "Letters to Lewald on the French Stage" found in Heine's Wit, Wisdom and Pathos *(Read by Thomas Banks in Podcast Ep. 62)*

Commonplace Quotes

"They say, a Carpenter's known by his Chips."
—Jonathan Swift in Polite Conversation in Three Dialogues *(Read by Thomas Banks in Podcast Ep. 61)*

"All too often, the legends old men tell are closer to the truth than the facts young professors tell. The wildest fairy tales of the ancients are far more realistic than the scientific phantasms imagined by moderns."
—Hilaire Belloc (Read by Angelina Stanford in Podcast Ep. 61)

Commonplace Quotes

"Earth's crammed with heaven,
And every common bush afire with God,
But only he who sees takes off his shoes…"
—Elizabeth Barrett Browning in "Aurora Leigh" (Read by Cindy Rollins in Podcast Ep. 61)

Commonplace Quotes

"The imagination of man is made in the image of the imagination of God. Everything of man must have been of God first; and it will help much towards our understanding of the imagination and its functions in man if we first succeed in regarding aright the imagination of God, in which the imagination of man lives and moves and has its being."

—George MacDonald "The Imagination: Its Functions and Its Culture" in A Dish of Orts

(Read by Cindy Rollins in Podcast Ep. 60)

"It is when a writer first begins to make enemies that he begins to matter."
—Hilton Brown in "Rudyard Kipling: a New Appreciation" (Read by Thomas Banks in Podcast Ep. 59)

Commonplace Quotes

"Kill that whence spring the crude fancies and wild day-dreams of the young, and you will never lead them beyond dull facts—dull because their relations to each other, and the one life that works in them all, must remain undiscovered. Whoever would have his children avoid this arid region will do well to allow no teacher to approach them—not even of mathematics—who has no imagination."

—George MacDonald in "The Imagination: Its Functions and Its Culture" in A Dish of Orts *(Read by Cindy Rollins in Podcast Ep. 59)*

Commonplace Quotes

"There were people who cared for him and people didn't, and those who didn't hate him were out to get him...But they couldn't touch him...because he was Tarzan, Mandrake, Flash Gordon. He was Bill Shakespeare. He was Cain, Ulysses, the Flying Dutchman; he was Lot in Sodom, Deidre of the Sorrows, Sweeney in the nightingales among trees."

—Joseph Heller in Catch-22 *(Read by Angelina Stanford in Podcast Ep. 59)*

Commonplace Quotes

"Here are some of the points which make a story worth studying to tell to the nestling listeners in many a sweet "Children's Hour";—graceful and artistic details; moral impulse of a high order, conveyed with a strong and delicate touch; sweet human affection; a tender, fanciful link between the children and the Nature-world; humour, pathos, righteous satire, and last, but not least, the fact that the story does not turn on children, and does not foster that self-consciousness, the dawn of which in the child is, perhaps, the individual "Fall of Man."

—Charlotte Mason in Formation of Character *(Read by Cindy Rollins in Podcast Ep. 58)*

Commonplace Quotes

"The essay began by noting that total war was underway, with fighting not only 'in the field and on the sea and in the air,' but also in 'the realm of ideas.' It said: 'The mightiest single weapon this war has yet employed' was 'not a plane, or a bomb or a juggernaut of tanks'—it was Mein Kampf. This single book caused an educated nation to 'burn the great books that keep liberty fresh in the hearts of men.' If America's goal was victory and world peace, 'all of us will have to know more and think better than our enemies think and know,' the council asserted. 'This is a war of books...Books are our weapons.'"

—Molly Guptill Manning, quoting from the essay "Books and the War" (Read by Angelina Stanford in Podcast Ep. 58)

"In everything I have sought peace and not found it, save in a corner with a book."
—Attributed to Thomas à Kempis (Read by Thomas Banks in Podcast Ep. 58)

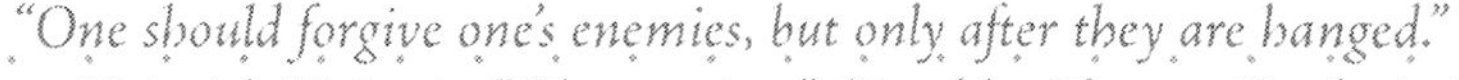

"One should forgive one's enemies, but only after they are hanged."
—Heinrich Heine in "Observations" (Read by Thomas Banks in Podcast Ep. 57)

Commonplace Quotes

"Human beings are not human doings."
—Nigel Goodwin, quoted by Makoto Fujimura in Culture Care *(Read by Cindy Rollins in Podcast Ep. 57)*

Commonplace Quotes

"But the object of my school is to show how many extraordinary things even a lazy and ordinary man may see, if he can spur himself to the single activity of seeing."
—G. K. Chesterton in "Tremendous Trifles" (Read by Thomas Banks in Podcast Ep. 56)

Commonplace Quotes

"Time can be both a threat and a friend to hope. Injustice, for example, has to be tediously dismantled, not exploded. This is often infuriating, but it is true."
—Makoto Fujimura in Culture Care *(Read by Cindy Rollins in Podcast Ep. 56)*

Commonplace Quotes

"The poet is traditionally a blind man, but the Christian poet, and story-teller as well, is like the blind man whom Christ touched, who looked then and saw men as if they were trees but walking. This is the beginning of vision, and it is an invitation to deeper and stranger visions than we shall have to learn to accept if we are to realize a truly Christian literature."

—Flannery O'Connor in Mystery and Manners *(Read by Angelina Stanford in Podcast Ep. 56)*

Commonplace Quotes

"To know God therefore as He is, is to frame the most beautiful idea in all worlds. He delighteth in our happiness more than we, and is of all others the most lovely object."
—Thomas Traherne in Centuries of Meditations *(Read by Thomas Banks in Podcast Ep. 55)*

Commonplace Quotes

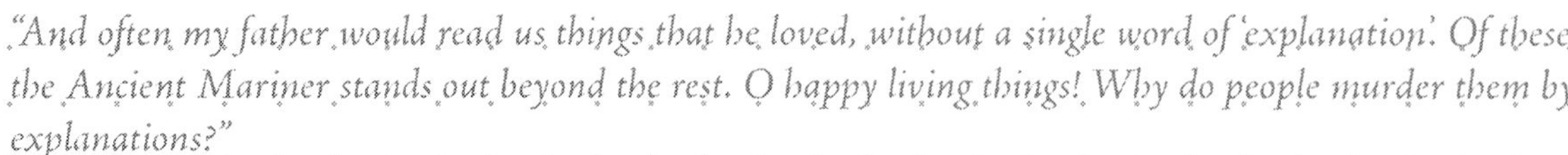

"And often my father would read us things that he loved, without a single word of 'explanation'. Of these the Ancient Mariner stands out beyond the rest. O happy living things! Why do people murder them by explanations?"

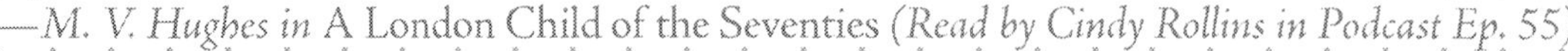

—M. V. Hughes in A London Child of the Seventies *(Read by Cindy Rollins in Podcast Ep. 55)*

Commonplace Quotes

"The mere fact that a story is a work of fiction, however, does not prevent its having a deep and significant truth of its own. We find, then, that the distinction between true stories and works of pure imagination, though convenient, is not quite essential. For fiction may be just as true, in the higher sense of the word, as history, or travel or any other record of actual experience."
—George Lyman Kittredge (Read by Angelina Stanford in Podcast Ep. 55)

Commonplace Quotes

"The knowledge-as-information vision is actually defective and damaging. It distorts reality and humanness, and it gets in the way of good knowing."

—Esther Lightcap Meek in A Little Manual of Knowing *(Read by Cindy Rollins in Podcast Ep. 54)*

"Perhaps it would be a good idea for public statues to be made with disposable heads that can be changed with popular fashion. But even better would surely be to make statues without any heads at all, representing simply the 'idea' of a good politician."
—Auberon Waugh in The Diaries of Auberon Waugh *(Read by Thomas Banks in Podcast Ep. 54)*

Commonplace Quotes

"When you can assume that your audience holds the same beliefs you do, you can relax a little and use more normal means of talking to it; when you have to assume that it does not, then you have to make your vision apparent by shock—to the hard of hearing you shout, and for the almost blind you use large and startling figures."
—Flannery O'Connor in Mystery and Manners *(Read by Angelina Stanford in Podcast Ep. 54)*

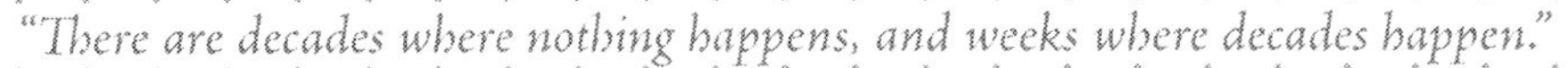

"There are decades where nothing happens, and weeks where decades happen."
—Attributed to Vladimir Lenin (Read by Thomas Banks in Podcast Ep. 53)

Commonplace Quotes

"While affording some secrets of 'the way of the will' to young people, we should perhaps beware of presenting the ideas of 'self-knowledge, self-reverence, and self-control.' All adequate education must be outward bound, and the mind which is concentrated upon self-emolument, even though it be the emolument of all the virtues, misses the higher and the simpler secrets of life. Duty and service are the sufficient motives for the arduous training of the will that a child goes through with little consciousness."

—*Charlotte Mason in* Towards a Philosophy of Education *(Read by Cindy Rollins in Podcast Ep. 53)*

Commonplace Quotes

"Perhaps the surest measure of O'Connor's sense of calling was her willingness to be misunderstood."
—*Jonathan Rogers in* The Terrible Speed of Mercy *(Read by Angelina Stanford in Podcast Ep. 53)*

Commonplace Quotes

"This the story of my life, that while I lived it weighed upon me and pressed against me and filled all my senses to overflowing and now is like a dream dreamed . . . This is my story, my giving of thanks."
—Wendell Berry in Hannah Coulter *(Read by Cindy Rollins in Podcast Ep. 52)*

Commonplace Quotes

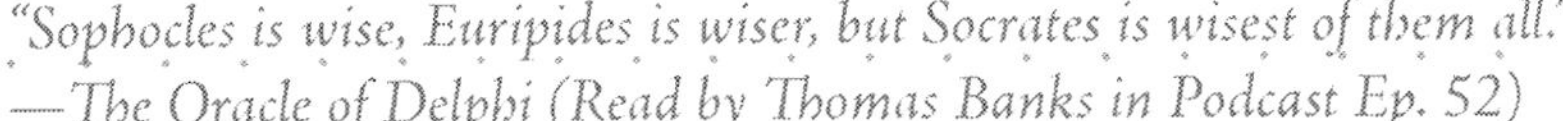
"Sophocles is wise, Euripides is wiser, but Socrates is wisest of them all."
—The Oracle of Delphi (Read by Thomas Banks in Podcast Ep. 52)

"The past is a foreign country: they do things differently there."
—*L. P. Hartley in* The Go-Between *(Read by Angelina Stanford in Podcast Ep. 52)*

Commonplace Quotes

"When we think of a friend, we do not count that a lost thought, though the friend never knew of it."
—John Donne in "Meditations" (Read by Thomas Banks in Podcast Ep. 51)

Commonplace Quotes

"'Oxford is,' Lewis said, 'a dangerous place for a book lover. Every second shop has something you want.' According to Warren Lewis, his brother soon learned to discipline such inclinations: 'In his younger days he was something of a bibliophile, but in middle and later life very seldom bought a book if he could consult it in the Bodleian: long years of poverty, self-inflicted but grinding, had made this economical habit second nature to him—a fact that contributed, no doubt, to the extra-ordinarily retentive character of his memory.'"
—*Clyde Kilby in* C.S. Lewis: Images of His World *(Read by Cindy Rollins in Podcast Ep. 51)*

Commonplace Quotes

"Children are always seeking out new experiences, and they find them in stories when adults do not spoil these stories by superimposing concepts or rules over the narrative."
—Vigen Guroian in "The Fairy Tale Wars" (Read by Angelina Stanford in Podcast Ep. 51)

Commonplace Quotes

"We chose from the library shelves any book of Tales for the Young, and took much pleasure in prophesying the events. We could rely on Providence to punish the naughty and bring to notice the heroism of the good, and generally grant an early death to both. Why was there a bull in a field? To gore the disobedient. Why did cholera break out? To kill the child who went down a forbidden street. The names told us much: Tom, Sam, or Jack were predestined to evil, while a Frank could do nothing but good. Henry was a bit uncertain: he might lead his little sister into that field with bravado, or he might attack the bull to save her life at the cost of his own. We had bettings of gooseberries on such points."

—M. V. Hughes in A London Child of the Seventies *(Read by Cindy Rollins in Podcast Ep. 50)*

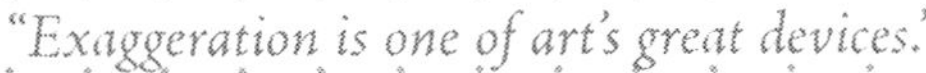

"Exaggeration is one of art's great devices."
—J. B. Priestley in "Papers from Lilliput" (Read by Thomas Banks in Podcast Ep. 50)

Commonplace Quotes

"Hell is inaccurate."
—Charles Williams, quoted in Preface to Paradise Lost *by C.S. Lewis (Read by Angelina Stanford in Podcast Ep. 50)*

Commonplace Quotes

"Meanwhile, you will write an essay on self-indulgence. There will be a prize of half a crown for the longest essay, irrespective of any possible merit."
—Evelyn Waugh in Decline and Fall *(Read by Thomas Banks in Podcast Ep. 49)*

Commonplace Quotes

"Shame belongs, rather, to the bookish recluse who knows not how to apply his reading to the good of his fellows or to manifest its fruit to the eyes of all."

—Cicero (Read by Angelina Stanford in Podcast Ep. 49)

"It is simply my lifelong experience—that men are more likely to hand over to others what they ought to do themselves, and women more likely to do themselves what others wish they would leave alone. Hence both sexes must be told 'Mind your own business,' but in two different senses!"
—*C. S. Lewis in* Letters to an American Lady *(Read by Cindy Rollins in Podcast Ep. 49)*

Commonplace Quotes

"We long for paradise because we were created for paradise. We were created to live in an environment that cooperates with, not fights against, our desires. We were created for Eden, a place we've never been, and so we desire a perfect life full of healthy relationships."

—*Julie Sparkman in* Unhitching from the Crazy Train: Finding Rest in a World You Can't Control *(Read by Cindy Rollins in Podcast Ep. 48)*

Commonplace Quotes

"Anyone who puts himself forward to be elected to a position of political power is almost bound to be socially or emotionally insecure, or criminally motivated, or mad."
—Auberon Waugh in The Diaries of Auberon Waugh *(Read by Thomas Banks in Podcast Ep. 48)*

Commonplace Quotes

"'The secret is not to dream,' she whispered, 'The secret is to wake up. Waking up is harder. I have woken up and now I am real. I know where I come from and where I'm going. You cannot fool me anymore. Or touch me. Or anything that is mine.'"

Terry Pratchett in Wee Free Men *(Read by Angelina Stanford in Podcast Ep. 48)*

Commonplace Quotes

"We do not obtain the most precious gifts by going in search of them but by waiting for them. Man cannot discover them by his own powers and if he sets out to seek for them he will find in their place counterfeits of which he will be unable to discern the falsity."

Simone Weil in Reflections on the Right Use of School Studies with a View to the Love of God *(Read by Cindy Rollins in Podcast Ep. 47)*

Commonplace Quotes

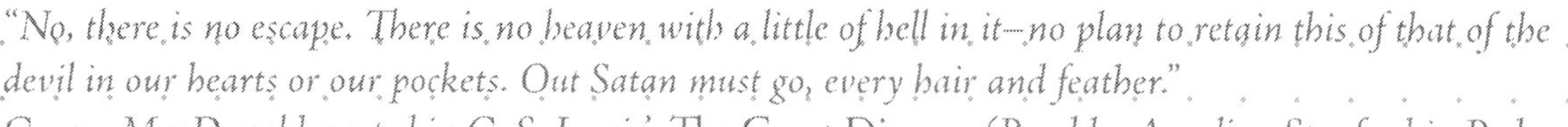

"No, there is no escape. There is no heaven with a little of hell in it—no plan to retain this of that of the devil in our hearts or our pockets. Out Satan must go, every hair and feather."
George MacDonald quoted in C. S. Lewis's The Great Divorce *(Read by Angelina Stanford in Podcast Ep. 47)*

Commonplace Quotes

"A poet is not a man who says 'look at me', but rather a man who points at something and says 'look at that.'"
C. S. *Lewis in* The Personal Heresy *(Read by Angelina Stanford in Podcast Ep. 47)*

Commonplace Quotes

"Wear your learning like your watch, in a private pocket; and do not pull it out and strike it merely to show that you have one."
—Lord Chesterfield, Letters *(Read by Thomas Banks in Podcast Ep. 46)*

Commonplace Quotes

"We must travel this path as lovers, amateurs, of the Word and of words because all things reveal themselves more truly to the eyes of love."
—Stratford Caldecott in Beauty in the Word *(Read by Angelina Stanford in Podcast Ep. 46)*

Commonplace Quotes

"Time's glory is to calm contending kings,
To unmask falsehood, and bring truth to light,
To stamp the seal of time in aged things,
To wake the morn and sentinel the night,
To wrong the wronger till he render right;
To ruinate proud buildings with thy hours,
And smear with dust their glittering golden towers."
—William Shakespeare "The Rape of Lucrece" (Read by Cindy Rollins in Podcast Ep. 46)

"About the lack of religious education: of course you must be grieved, but remember how much religious education has exactly the opposite effect to that which was intended, how many hard atheists come from pious homes. May we not hope, with God's mercy, that a similarly opposite effect may be produced in her case? Parents are not Providence: their bad intentions may be frustrated as their good ones."

—C. S. Lewis *in* Letters to an American Lady (*Read by Cindy Rollins in Podcast Ep. 45*)

Commonplace Quotes

"It is faintly amusing when one reads about society lapsing back into paganism. I, for one, would think it rather a picturesque incident if the Prime Minister were to sacrifice an ox in the temple of Venus."
—C. S. Lewis (Read by Thomas Banks in Podcast Ep. 45)

Commonplace Quotes

"Hell is a state of mind – ye never said a truer word. And every state of mind, left to itself, every shutting up of the creature within the dungeon of its own mind – is, in the end, Hell. But Heaven is not a state of mind. Heaven is reality itself. All that is fully real is Heavenly. For all that can be shaken will be shaken and only the unshakeable remains."

—*C. S. Lewis in* The Great Divorce *(Read by Angelina Stanford in Podcast Ep. 45)*

Commonplace Quotes

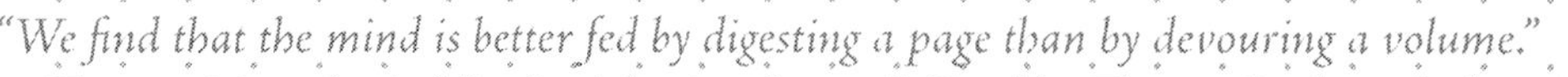

"We find that the mind is better fed by digesting a page than by devouring a volume."

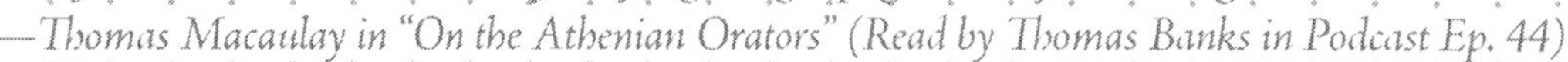

—Thomas Macaulay in "On the Athenian Orators" (Read by Thomas Banks in Podcast Ep. 44)

"Education is an admirable thing. But it is well to remember from time to time that nothing that is worth knowing can be taught."
—Oscar Wilde in Intentions *(Read by Angelina Stanford in Podcast Ep. 44)*

Commonplace Quotes

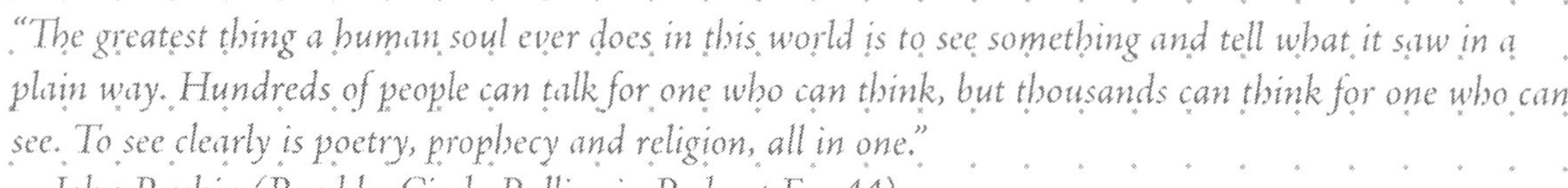

"The greatest thing a human soul ever does in this world is to see something and tell what it saw in a plain way. Hundreds of people can talk for one who can think, but thousands can think for one who can see. To see clearly is poetry, prophecy and religion, all in one."
—John Ruskin (Read by Cindy Rollins in Podcast Ep. 44)

Commonplace Quotes

"For your face I have exchanged all faces."
—Philip Larkin in "To My Wife" (Read by Thomas Banks in Podcast Ep. 43)

"Just as conscience, or the moral sense, recognizes duty; just as the intellect deals with the truth; so is it the part of taste alone to form us of BEAUTY. And Poesy is the handmaiden but of Taste. Yet we would not be misunderstood. This handmaiden is not forbidden to moralize—in her own fashion. She is not forbidden to depict—but to reason and preach, of virtue. As, of this latter, conscience recognizes the obligation, so intellect teaches the expediency, while taste contents herself with displaying the beauty waging war with vice merely on the ground of its inconsistency with fitness, harmony, proportion—in a word with beauty."

—Edgar Allan Poe in Review of Longfellow's Ballads and Other Poems *(Read by Angelina Stanford in Podcast Ep. 43)*

Commonplace Quotes

"Whatever happens will be for the worse, and therefore it is in our interest that as little should happen as possible."
—Lord Salisbury (Read by Thomas Banks in Podcast Ep. 37)

"An important part of a child's education is storytelling, since good stories excite the imagination and strengthen the bond between parent and child."
—St. John Chrysostom (Read by Angelina Stanford in Podcast Ep. 42)

Book Reviews

My Review

Title: ***Date Read:***
Author: ***Rating:*** ☆ ☆ ☆ ☆ ☆

My Review

Title:

Author:

Date Read:

Rating: ☆ ☆ ☆ ☆ ☆

My Review

Title:
Author:

Date Read:
Rating: ☆ ☆ ☆ ☆ ☆

My Review

Title:

Author:

Date Read:

Rating: ☆ ☆ ☆ ☆ ☆

My Review

Title:
Author:

Date Read:
Rating: ☆ ☆ ☆ ☆ ☆

My Review

Title:
Author:

Date Read:
Rating: ☆ ☆ ☆ ☆ ☆

My Review

Title:
Date Read:
Author:
Rating: ☆ ☆ ☆ ☆ ☆

My Review

Title:

Author:

Date Read:

Rating: ☆ ☆ ☆ ☆ ☆

My Review

Title:

Author:

Date Read:

Rating: ☆ ☆ ☆ ☆ ☆

My Review

Title:
Author:

Date Read:
Rating: ☆ ☆ ☆ ☆ ☆

My Review

Title:
Author:

Date Read:
Rating: ☆ ☆ ☆ ☆ ☆

My Review

Title:

Author:

Date Read:

Rating: ☆ ☆ ☆ ☆ ☆

My Review

Title:
Author:

Date Read:
Rating: ☆ ☆ ☆ ☆ ☆

My Review

Title:
Author:

Date Read:
Rating: ☆ ☆ ☆ ☆ ☆

My Review

Title:
Author:

Date Read:
Rating: ☆ ☆ ☆ ☆ ☆

My Review

Title:
Author:

Date Read:
Rating: ☆ ☆ ☆ ☆ ☆

My Review

Title:

Author:

Date Read:

Rating: ☆ ☆ ☆ ☆ ☆

My Review

Title:
Author:

Date Read:
Rating: ☆ ☆ ☆ ☆ ☆

My Review

Title:
Author:

Date Read:
Rating: ☆ ☆ ☆ ☆ ☆

My Review

Title:

Author:

Date Read:

Rating: ☆ ☆ ☆ ☆ ☆

My Review

Title:
Author:

Date Read:
Rating: ☆ ☆ ☆ ☆ ☆

My Review

Title:
Author:

Date Read:
Rating: ☆ ☆ ☆ ☆ ☆

My Review

Title:

Author:

Date Read:

Rating: ☆ ☆ ☆ ☆ ☆

My Review

Title:
Author:

Date Read:
Rating: ☆ ☆ ☆ ☆ ☆

What will you read for the challenge?

It's entirely up to you, of course! That's the fun! But sometimes it might be hard to think of something good for a particular category. So we'll throw out a few titles to get you started...

A Poetry Anthology

Anything from Mother Goose to "Q" (*Oxford Book of English Verse* by Sir Arthur Quiller-Couch)
Favorite Poems Old and New edited by Helen Ferris
100 Best Poems of All Time edited by Leslie Pockell
Lyrical Ballads by Coleridge and Wordsworth
Immortal Poems of the English Language edited by Oscar Williams

A Book (or Selection) of Letters

The Habit of Being by Flannery O'Connor
Letters to an American Lady by C.S. Lewis
Letters to Children by C.S. Lewis
84, Charing Cross Road by Helene Hanff
P.G. Wodehouse: A Life in Letters edited by Sophie Ratcliffe
The Letters of John and Abigail Adams edited by Frank Shuffelton (Penguin Classics)
Selected Letters of Jane Austen edited by Vivien Jones (Oxford World's Classics)

A Book From Your To-Be-Read Stack

See pages 16-19. This one is up to you!

An Ancient Greek or Roman Work (A Play, Epic, or Collection of Myths)

Agamemnon by Aeschylus
Antigone by Sophocles
The Clouds by Aristophanes
The Illiad by Homer
The Aeneid by Virgil
Metamorphoses by Ovid
D'Aulaire's *Book of Greek Myths*
Bulfinch's Mythology by Thomas Bulfinch
Mythology: Timeless Tales of Gods and Heroes by Edith Hamilton

A Book on Education, Art, or Literature

Beauty in the Word: Rethinking the Foundations of Education by Stratford Caldecott
Norms and Nobility by David Hicks
Mind of the Maker by Dorothy Sayers
On Reading Well by Karen Swallow Prior
The Meaning of Shakespeare by Harold Goddard
The Educated Imagination by Northrop Frye

Founders of the Middle Ages by E.K. Rand
The Discarded Image by C.S. Lewis
The Year of our Lord 1943: Christian Humanism in an Age of Crisis by Alan Jacobs
Culture Care: Reconnecting with Beauty for Our Common Life by Makoto Fujimura

A Victorian Novel

Silas Marner by George Eliot
Middlemarch by George Eliot
North and South by Elizabeth Gaskell
Great Expectations by Charles Dickens
The Count of Monte Cristo by Alexandre Dumas
The Black Arrow by Robert Louis Stevenson
The Warden by Anthony Trollope
Vanity Fair by William Makepeace Thackeray
George MacDonald novels

A Lesser-Known Book by a Well-Known Author

The Personal Heresy by C.S. Lewis
Holy War by John Bunyan
Villette by Charlotte Bronte
"Leaf by Niggle" by J.R.R Tolkien
Adam Bede by George Eliot
The White Company by Sir Arthur Conan Doyle
The Secret Agent by Joseph Conrad
Ruth by Elizabeth Gaskell

A Shakespeare Play

Will it be a comedy or a tragedy? There are only so many to choose from . . . you've got this!

A Book You Have Avoided

What are you avoiding?

Finish a Book You Started but Never Finished

We don't know for sure what you might choose here, but maybe it's . . .
Les Miserables by Victor Hugo
Kristin Lavransdatter by Sigrid Undset
Anna Karenina by Leo Tolstoy
The Fellowship of the Ring by J.R.R. Tolkien
Till We Have Faces by C.S. Lewis

A Literary Biography

Life of Samuel Johnson by James Boswell
The Narnian by Alan Jacobs (Biography of C.S. Lewis)
J.R.R. Tolkien a Biography by Humphrey Carpenter
Jane Austen: A Life by Clair Tomalin
Dorothy Sayers: Her Life & Soul by Barbara Reynolds
Bandersnatch: C.S. Lewis, J.R.R. Tolkien, and the Creative Collaboration of the Inklings by Diana Pavlac Glyer, illustrated by James A. Owen
Winston Churchill by Paul Johnson
A Study of George Orwell: the Man and His Works by Christopher Hollis
The Life of Charlotte Brontë by Elizabeth Gaskell
The Terrible Speed of Mercy by Jonathan Rogers
An Autobiography by Agatha Christie
An Autobiography and Other Writings by Anthony Trollope
Milton by Rose Macaulay
Chaucer by G.K. Chesterton
Napoleon by Paul Johnson
Julius Caesar by John Buchan

Something Russian (A Play, Short Story, Novel, or Novella)

Anna Karenina by Leo Tolstoy
War & Peace by Leo Tolstoy
Crime & Punishment by Fyodor Dostoevsky
The Death of Ivan Ilych by Leo Tolstoy
One Day in the Life of Ivan Denisovich by Alexander Solhenitsyn
Harvard Address Given in 1978 by Alexander Solhenitsyn
The Cherry Orchard by Anton Chekhov
Onegin by Pushkin (quite easy)
Fathers and Sons by Ivan Turgenev

A Regional or Local Book

A book related in some way to your local area. We don't know where you are, naturally, but here are some titles known for their settings:

East Coast
A Tree Grows in Brooklyn by Betty Smith
The Chosen or *My Name is Asher Lev* by Chaim Potok
South
Flannery O' Connor stories
Christy by Catherine Marshall
Kate Chopin's stories
Wendell Berry's novels
Cold Sassy Tree by Olive Ann Burns
Penhally by Caroline Gordon

Midwest
My Ántonia by Willa Cather
Little House on the Prairie books by Laura Ingalls Wilder
The Trees, The Fields, and *The Town* (trilogy) by Conrad Richter
Booth Tarkington's novels or stories
Upper Midwest
Peace like a River by Leif Engler
Betsy-Tacy book series by Maud Hart Lovelace
A Lantern in her Hand by Bess Streeter Aldrich
West
Little Britches by Ralph Moody
Zane Grey novels, such as *Riders of the Purple Sage*
Giants in the Earth: A Saga of the Prairie by O.E. Rolvaag
Lilies of the Field by Willam Edmund Barrett
California
Ramona by Helen Hunt Jackson
East of Eden by John Steinbeck
The Big Sleep by Raymond Chandler
The Lonesome Gods by Louis L'Amour

A 14th, 15th, or 16th Century Book

A book written in, set in, or about those centuries:
Faerie Queene by Edmund Spenser
Ivanhoe by Walter Sir Scott
The Scottish Chiefs by Jane Porter
"York Play of the Crucifixion" (and other mystery plays)
"The Everyman" (play)
Sir Gawain and the Green Knight translated by Burton Raffel
A Distant Mirror by Barbara Tuchman
The Imitation of Christ by Thomas à Kempis

A Book in a Genre You Don't Normally Read

The Scarlet Pimpernel by Baroness Orzy
How the Irish Saved Civilization by Thomas Cahill
Journey into Fear by Eric Ambler
Oxford Time Travel books, such as *Doomsday Book,* by Connie Willis

An Obscure Book Mentioned by Thomas Banks

Or any book mentioned on the podcast. We know how quickly your To-Be-Read pile grows when you listen to the podcast. Pick a book mentioned on the podcast to read for this category.
The Stories That Helped Us Win World War II by Molly Guptill Manning (Episode 57)
The Characters of Shakespeare's Plays by William Hazlett (Ep. 38)
The Lays of Ancient Rome by Thomas Macaulay (Ep. 44)

On Three Ways of Writing for Children by C. S. Lewis (Ep. 70)
The Elizabethan World Picture by E. M. Tillyard (Ep.34)
Imaginary Conversations by Walter Savage Landor

A Light Comedic Novel

P.G. Wodehouse novels
Miss Pettigrew Lives For a Day by Winifred Watson
Belgravia by Julian Fellowes
Miss Buncle's Book by D.E. Stevenson
The Autobiography of a Cad by A.G. Macdonell

An "Other World" Book

("Other world" in the literary sense. A fantasy or sci-fi book.)

The Space Trilogy of C.S. Lewis
The Lord of the Rings by J.R.R. Tolkien
The Chronicles of Narnia by C.S. Lewis
Phantastes by George MacDonald
20,000 Leagues under the Sea by Jules Verne
The Time Machine by H.G. Wells
War of the Worlds by H.G. Wells

A Travel Book

Travels with a Donkey in the Cevennes by R. L. Stevenson
A Walk in the Woods: Rediscovering America on the Appalachian Trail by Bill Bryson
A Year in Provence by Peter Mayle
My Family and Other Animals by Gerald Durrell
What I Saw in America by G.K. Chesterton
The Lawless Roads by Graham Greene
Down and Out in Paris and London by George Orwell
A Moveable Feast by Ernest Hemingway
The Flame Trees of Thika by Elsbeth Huxley

About the Authors

Angelina Stanford

Angelina Stanford has an Honors Baccalaureate Degree and a Master's Degree in English Literature from the University of Louisiana, graduating Phi Kappa Phi. For over twenty-five years, she has shared her passion and enthusiasm for literature with students in a variety of settings and is a popular conference speaker and podcast guest. In 2020, with her husband, Thomas Banks, she founded the House of Humane Letters, providing classes, webinars, conferences and other resources for a more humane education. Angelina maintains a high commitment to teaching teachers and students the skill and art of reading well—and in recapturing the tradition of literary scholarship needed to fully engage with the Great Books. She is a great believer that Stories Will Save the World!

Cindy Rollins

Cindy Rollins homeschooled her nine children for over thirty years. She is a co-host with Angelina Stanford and Thomas Banks of the popular Literary Life Podcast and curates the "Over the Back Fence Newsletter" at CindyRollins.net. She is the author of *Mere Motherhood: Morning Time, Nursery Rhymes, and My Journey Toward Sanctification; A Handbook for Morning Time*; the *Mere Motherhood Newsletters*; and *Hallelujah: Cultivating Advent Traditions with Handel's Messiah.*

Cindy runs an active Patreon group where the participants read Charlotte Mason's volumes and discuss questions pertaining to motherhood and life. Her heart's desire is to encourage moms using Charlotte Mason's timeless principles. She lives in Chattanooga, Tennessee, with her husband, Tim, and dog, Max. She also travels around the country visiting her 13 grandchildren, watching her youngest son play baseball, and occasionally speaking at events.

Thomas Banks

Thomas Banks has taught great books with an emphasis on Greek and Roman literature, Latin grammar and ancient history for more than ten years both as a private tutor and as a junior high and high school teacher in his native Idaho and Montana. He holds a dual bachelor's degree in English Literature and Classical Studies from the University of Idaho, from which he graduated in 2008. In the summer of 2019, he moved to North Carolina to marry the illustrious Ms. Angelina Stanford, who said yes for some reason.

Poetry is a particular love of his, and he has published original verse and translations in First Things, the St. Austin Review and various other periodicals. His personal list of favorite writers never really stops growing, but will always include Homer, Euripides, Virgil, Ovid, St. Augustine, Shakespeare, Samuel Johnson, Byron, Keats, Walter Scott and Thomas Hardy. Of these and so many others one cannot have enough.

Thomas Banks currently resides in North Carolina, where he teaches Latin, literature and history online with his wife Angelina Stanford at The House of Humane Letters. His poetry, translations and other writings have appeared in First Things, The Imaginative Conservative, The New English Review, and various other publications.

Other Blue Sky Daisies Titles

Geography Books

**Elementary Geography* by Charlotte Mason

**Home Geography for Primary Grades with Written and Oral Exercises* by C. C. Long

Language Arts and Grammar Books

**The Mother Tongue: Adapted for Modern Students* by George Lyman Kittredge. In this series: Workbook 1 and 2; Answer Key 1 and 2

Exercises in Dictation by F. Peel

**Grammar Land: Grammar in Fun for the Children of Schoolroom Shire (Annotated)* By M. L. Nesbitt. Annotated by Amy M. Edwards and Christina J. Mugglin

The CopyWorkBook Series

The CopyWorkBook: George Washington's Rules of Civility & Decent Behavior in Company and Conversation by Amy M. Edwards and Christina J. Mugglin

The CopyWorkBook: Comedies of William Shakespeare by Amy M. Edwards and Christina J. Mugglin

Other Titles

Hallelujah: Cultivating Advent Traditions with Handel's Messiah by Cindy Rollins

The Birds' Christmas Carol by Kate Douglas Wiggin

The Innkeeper's Daughter by Michelle Lallement

Kipling's Rikki-Tikki-Tavi: A Children's Play by Amy M. Edwards

*These titles are popular with those inspired by Charlotte Mason and her educational philosophy.

Made in the USA
Middletown, DE
08 September 2021